STAYING SAFE
ONLINE

Steffi Cavell-Clarke & Thomas Welch

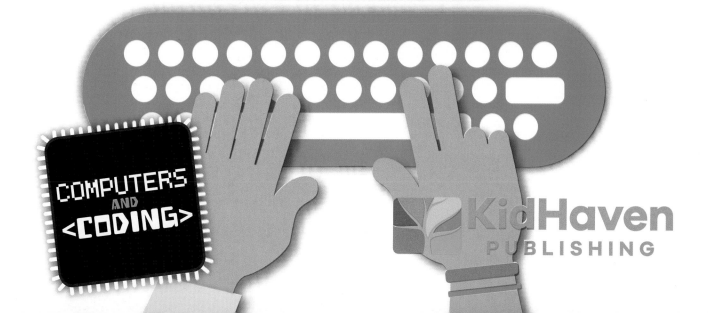

COMPUTERS AND <CODING>

KidHaven
PUBLISHING

Published in 2019 by KidHaven Publishing, an Imprint of Greenhaven Publishing, LLC
353 3rd Avenue, Suite 255, New York, NY 10010

Written by: Steffi Cavell-Clarke & Thomas Welch
Edited by: Kirsty Holmes
Designed by: Danielle Jones

Cataloging-in-Publication Data

Names: Cavell-Clarke, Steffi. | Welch, Thomas.
Title: Staying safe online / Steffi Cavell-Clarke & Thomas Welch.
Description: New York : KidHaven Publishing, 2019. | Series: Computers and coding | Includes glossary and index.
Identifiers: ISBN 9781534527126 (pbk.) | ISBN 9781534527119 (library bound) | ISBN 9781534527133 (6 pack)
Subjects: LCSH: Internet--Safety measures--Juvenile literature. | Internet and children--Juvenile literature.
Classification: LCC TK5105.875.I57 C38 2019 | DDC 004.67'8083--dc23

IMAGE CREDITS

**Abbreviations: l-left, r-right, b-bottom,
t-top, c-centre, m-middle.**

Cover – izabel.l, 1000s_pixels, Macrovector, danjazzia. 4 – vladwel, peiyang. 5 – Sudowoodo , Inspiring, Oceans, johavel. 6 – Sudowoodo, SofiaV,
Top Vector Studio. 7 – Sudowoodo, T-Kot, KittyVector. 8 – Sudowoodo, Cartoon Industry. 9 – Sudowoodo, Rzt Moster, 1000s_pixels. 10 – Sudowoodo,
MSSA. 11 – Sudowoodo, Inspiring. 12 – Sudowoodo, BarsRsind, Lemberg Vector studio. 13 – Sudowoodo, HieroGraphic. 14 – stokk, Sudowoodo.
16 – girafchik, ivleva1975, hanss, Sudowoodo. 17 – Elvetica, Sudowoodo. 18 – Sudowoodo, flower travelin' man, Olga Sudowoodo, Lebedeva,
VasutinSergey. 19 – Sudowoodo, Mushakesa. 20 – paitoon, Sudowoodo. 21 – Sudowoodo, Mascha Tace. 22–23 – Julia Tim.
Images are courtesy of Shutterstock.com. With thanks to Getty Images, Thinkstock Photo and iStockphoto.

Printed in the United States of America

CPSIA compliance information: Batch # BS18KL: For further information contact Greenhaven Publishing LLC, New York, New York at 1-844-317-7404.

STAYING SAFE ONLINE

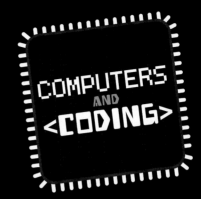

COMPUTERS
AND
<CODING>

Words that look like **this** can be found in the glossary on page 24.

USING THE INTERNET

The Internet is a **network** of lots and lots of computers that are connected to each other. This means that people from all over the world can **communicate** with each other.

DID YOU KNOW?

Over three **billion** people use the Internet.

4

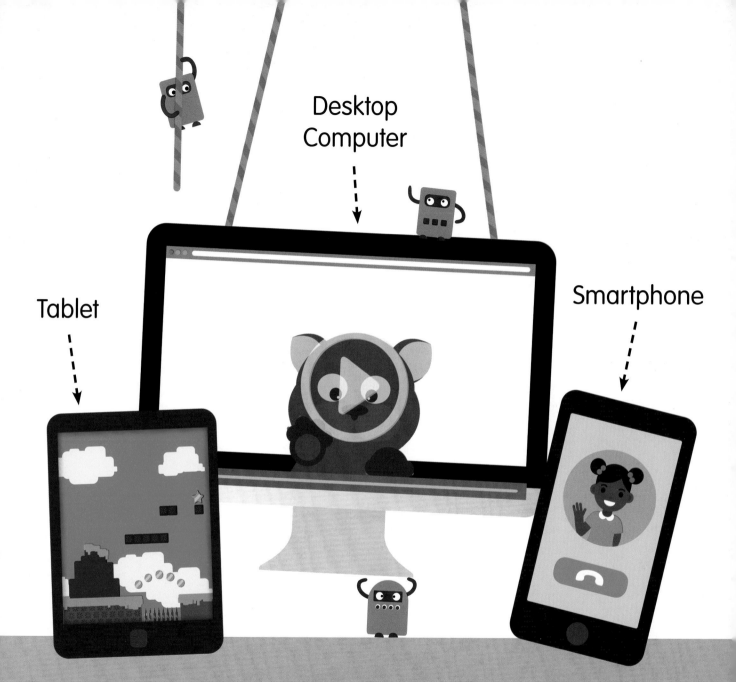

Tablet

Desktop
Computer

Smartphone

You can use the Internet on computers, tablets, and phones.
The Internet can help you to do lots of things, such as watch
funny videos, talk to friends who are far away, or play games.

5

BEING SAFE
ONLINE

Being "online" means that you are using the Internet. Just like in real life, you need to make sure that you are safe when you are online. There are lots of things that you can do to make sure that you are safe.

The most important thing you can do to stay safe online is to make sure that your parents or caregivers know that you are using the Internet. Agree on the **websites** that you can visit and the times when you can use the Internet.

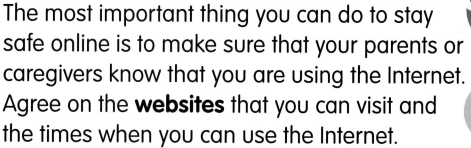

REMEMBER
Always let a **responsible** adult know when you are online.

WHY IS IT IMPORTANT TO BE SAFE?

Sometimes people behave differently online from how they would behave in person. Some people may do or say things that upset you, so it is important that you can talk to a responsible adult, like a parent or a teacher.

Parent

Teacher

Some websites are not for children. It's important to let an adult know what you are doing on the Internet so that they can make sure it is safe.

SHARING PERSONAL INFORMATION

Personal information tells other people who you are and where to find you. This includes your name, address, school, and what you look like. You should not share this kind of information with people you do not know.

If someone asks for your information, they might not always want to be your friend. They might want your information to use for other reasons. They might even want to hurt you.

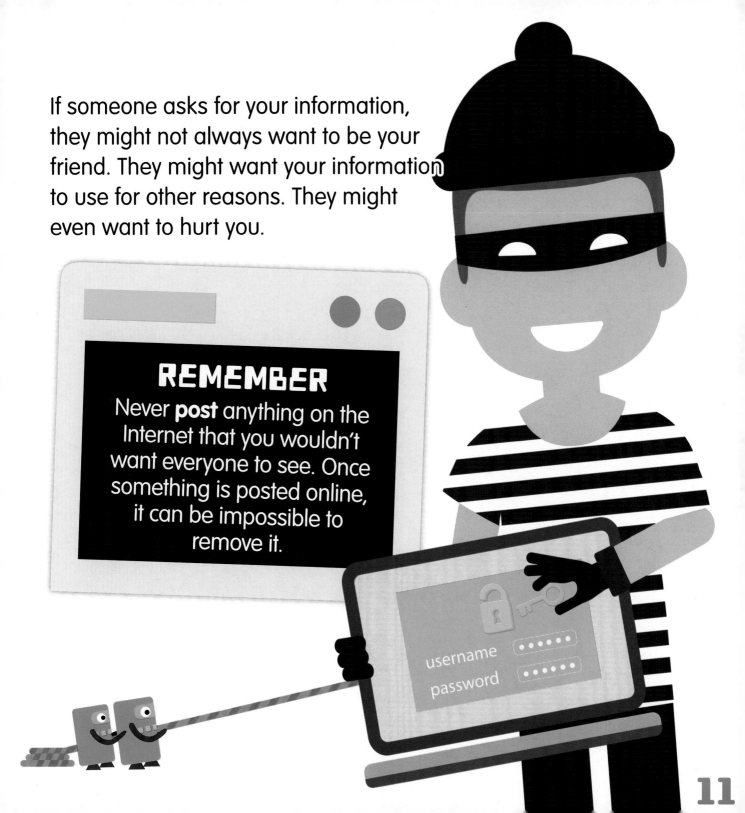

REMEMBER
Never **post** anything on the Internet that you wouldn't want everyone to see. Once something is posted online, it can be impossible to remove it.

username
password

SECURITY AND
PASSWORDS

You will need a **username** and **password** to use some websites and play online games. Passwords keep your accounts **secure**. This means that no one else can use your account.

USERNAME

****

SIGN IN

Never share your password with anybody else, other than the adults who look after you. If you share your password, you might be at risk of others logging in to your account and pretending to be you, or doing things you might not like.

SAFE WEBSITES

We use the Internet to access the World Wide Web, which is made up of millions of websites. A website is made up of webpages. A webpage can have videos, pictures, words, and games on it. Each webpage has a web address, which tells you all the information you need to find the webpage. Different parts of a web address tell us different things.

https://www.greenhavenpublishing.com/products

The name of the way webpages are sent to your computer. The "s" at the end means it has been sent securely.

Stands for World Wide Web.

Shows the company, school, or organization.

Shows the section of the web that the page is stored in.

The specific webpage

Some websites have pictures or videos that can make you feel worried or scared. Ask an adult that you trust before you use a website so that you know it is safe.

REMEMBER

Think before you click!

15

ONLINE
RELATIONSHIPS

Many people use the Internet to chat with their friends or make new friends. The friendships you make online can seem very real, but they are not the same as the friendships you make in day-to-day life.

We usually cannot see who we are talking to over the Internet. This means that it can be hard to tell if a person is who they say they are.

Never go alone to meet someone you have met online. If you really want to meet them, always take a parent or caregiver with you and go to a safe place where there are other people.

PEER PRESSURE

Sometimes, even friends try to make you do things you don't want to do. This is called peer pressure. Peer pressure can happen online, too. You might be asked to post a photo or comment, even though you don't want to.

If someone asks you to do something that you don't want to do, tell a responsible adult and they will help you. Once you post photos or videos online, it can be difficult to remove them, so never post anything you wouldn't want anyone else to see.

CYBERBULLYING

Cyberbullying means using the Internet to hurt, scare, or embarrass other people. Sharing private photos, posting nasty comments, and sending hurtful messages are all examples of cyberbullying.

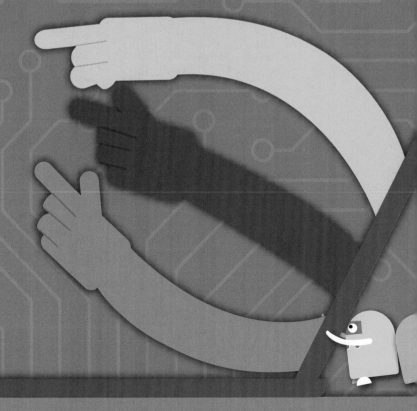

Even if you think someone was mean to you, you shouldn't be mean back. Instead, get help from an adult you trust. Always speak up if you notice anyone cyberbullying. Never keep it a secret.

TOP TIPS FOR

THINK BEFORE YOU POST

Don't upload or share anything you wouldn't want your parents, teachers, or friends to see. Once you press "send," it is no longer private. You can't be sure who will end up seeing it.

BE CAREFUL WHO YOU CHAT WITH

Remember that not everyone online is who they say they are. Never go alone to meet someone you have met online. Always take an adult.

ONLINE SAFETY

○ **BE CAREFUL WHAT YOU SHARE ONLINE**
Never post personal information online, like your address or telephone number.

○ **KEEP IT PRIVATE**
Always remember to keep your passwords private and make them difficult for other people to guess.

Password
* * * * _

GLOSSARY

BILLION	one thousand million
COMMUNICATE	to pass information between two or more people
NETWORK	a system of connected people or things
PASSWORD	a secret word that must be used to get into a place
POST	upload something online
RESPONSIBLE	trusted to do the right thing
SECURE	safe
USERNAME	an online identity
WEBSITES	pages of information on the Internet

INDEX